LIKE A

KISS on the LIPS

RESOURCES BY LES AND LESLIE PARROTT

Books

Becoming Soul Mates
Like a Kiss on the Lips
The Marriage Mentor Manual
Questions Couples Ask
Saving Your Marriage Before It Starts
Saving Your Marriage Before It Starts Workbook for Men
Saving Your Marriage Before It Starts Workbook for Women

Video Curriculum

Mentoring Engaged and Newlywed Couples
Saving Your Marriage Before It Starts

Audio Pages

Saving Your Marriage Before It Starts

Books by Les Parrott III

Helping the Struggling Adolescent
High Maintenance Relationships
Love's Unseen Enemy

LIKE A
KISS on
the LIPS

Meditations on Proverbs for Couples

Les & Leslie PARROTT

ZondervanPublishingHouse
Grand Rapids, Michigan

A Division of HarperCollinsPublishers

Like a Kiss on the Lips
Copyright © 1997 by Les and Leslie Parrott

Requests for information should be addressed to:

📖 ZondervanPublishingHouse
Grand Rapids, Michigan 49530

Library of Congress Cataloging-in-Publication Data

Parrott, Les.
    Like a kiss on the lips : meditations on proverbs for couples / Les and Leslie Parrott.
        p.   cm.
    ISBN: 0-310-21623-0 (hardcover)
    1. Married people—Religious life.   2. Marriage—Meditations.   I. Parrott, Leslie L., 1964–   . II. Title.
BV4596.M3P375   1997
242'.644—dc21   97-3352
                                                                                  CIP

This edition is printed on acid-free paper and meets the American National Standards Institute Z39.48 standard.

Interior Design by Jody DeNeef

Printed in the United States of America

97 98 99 00 01 02 03 /❖ DC/ 10 9 8 7 6 5 4 3 2 1

To Steve and Thanne Moore
Neighbors, friends, and a couple who
shares our love of practical Proverbs

Contents

Acknowledgments

Proverbs are simply platitudes until you have personally experienced the truth of them. And we have experienced the truth of "giving without sparing" from everyone involved in this project. Scott Bolinder, Stan Gundry, Sandy Vander Zicht, Lori Walburg, John Topliff, Greg Stielstra, Joyce Ondersma, and many others at Zondervan have given us support and encouragement at every turn while writing this book. Our hearts are also filled with special gratitude to Janice Lundquist for her unswerving dedication to helping us spread the good news. We are indebted to all of you.

Introduction

A thousand years before Christ was born, the wisest man in Israel's history, King Solomon, made his mark by leaving behind a body of wisdom unparalleled in the ancient world. Through his writings, Solomon intended to teach his readers how to live a truly meaningful life. Three thousand years later, Proverbs—Solomon's book of short, sharp phrases—is among the most widely read books in the Old Testament.

It is no surprise, then, that in Proverbs you will find practical wisdom to help you apply God's principles of living to virtually every area of married life—communication, money, sex, commitment, recreation, forgiveness, anger, humility, and conflict, to name a few. A book of ancient learning, Proverbs is still as contemporary as the latest bestseller on marriage.

Read through bits of Proverbs, and you'll find it hard to believe that the words were written so many years ago. Proverbs includes streetwise, no-nonsense advice in a variety of literary forms, from poems and parables to pointed questions and couplets. It is not a list of complicated rules to govern every move. Rather, it is a collection of truths to help us make the right decisions and lead more meaningful, happy lives.

Proverbs is best digested a few sayings at a time. And in this little book we have selected some of the most salient passages for married couples to ponder. Most importantly, these wise sayings must be talked about. Read them aloud together. Commit a few to memory. And fill your marriage with wise and good conversation.

—Les and Leslie Parrott

1

Like a Kiss on the Lips 2/24

An honest answer is like a kiss on the lips
—Proverbs 24:26

*O*f all the little expressions of love—a box of choco-lates, a handwritten poem, or a bouquet of handpicked wild-flowers—I think my favorite is a good old-fashioned kiss on the lips. Whether it be the gratuitous kind that comes with greeting my husband after a day at work or his surprising ambush kiss while standing in line at the grocery, I always feel especially loved when Les gives me a simple kiss.

Did you know the word *kiss* comes from a prehistoric syllable that is believed to be the sound of kissing? However the word originated and whoever named it really doesn't mat-ter to me. I just know I like kisses. And why shouldn't I? Kiss-es, according to a Danish saying, are the messengers of love.

No wonder then that Solomon, in all his wisdom, equaled a kiss on the lips to an honest answer. Love cannot last without honesty. Our honest answers create trust, the very bedrock of a relationship.

Every couple tells little white lies to one another in an attempt to be more loving. If we don't like our partner's cook-ing, for example, we might say, "Oh, it's wonderful." A little lie won't hurt our relationship, will it? Wrong.

Consider Ron and Cindy who had been married only a few weeks when he cooked his famous barbecue ribs on their brand new grill. As they were eating, Ron asked Cindy if she liked the ribs. Cindy knew Ron had worked hard to make them and was afraid that she would offend him if she was honest. "Oh, yes," she told Ron, "they're great!"

Believing that Cindy really liked his famous dish, Ron began barbecuing quite regularly, and there were always leftovers which had to be eaten. After a while, Cindy could bear it no longer, and in a moment of anger about something else she confessed that his barbecued ribs made her gag and she never wanted to see them on her table again! Ron was shocked and hurt. She had lied to him. "How can I ever believe you again?" he asked.

Should Cindy have told Ron right from the beginning that the ribs made her gag? Not if she cared about her marriage. Honesty does not require brutality. Truth is brutal only when it is a partial truth or when it is meant to cause pain. To be both honest and loving, she could say something like, "Not really, I've never liked barbecue on the grill—but I love seeing you cook."

The tragedy of most small deceptions is that they mushroom, ultimately creating a cloud of distrust that hovers over a relationship. Surely that's what was on King Solomon's mind when he wrote this proverb. So take his advice and whenever possible kiss your spouse on the lips with honesty.

🌿 To Ponder 🌿

- Consider a time when you told a white lie to avoid hurting your spouse's feelings. What was the result? Could you have handled the situation better by being honest?

- Oliver Wendell Holmes said, "The sound of a kiss is not so loud as that of a cannon, but its echo lasts a great deal longer." In what ways is an honest answer the same way?

2

Happily Ever Laughter

> *Like a madman shooting firebrands*
> *or deadly arrows is a man who deceives his*
> *neighbor and says, "I was only joking!"*
> —Proverbs 26:18–19

Leslie and I were in the middle of a joint project and had just resolved a small tiff about my being more patient with her work style. She is process-oriented, relational, and unruffled, while I am task-oriented, sequential, and eager when tackling a project. And because I push myself hard most of the time, I tend to push others, including my wife, and can become irritatingly impatient.

We had just resolved this squabble, or so we thought, when the following words tumbled out of my mouth: "Can't you pick up the pace a little here? We're never going to meet our deadline at this rate!"

Leslie looked at me in sheer amazement, made a quick study of my facial expression, determined I was serious, and burst into tears.

I would have done anything to rewind the clock thirty seconds. I winced, but I couldn't deny that my true feelings had seeped out, and I could do little to retract the words that had given me away. Or could I? In a vain attempt to do just

17

that, I resorted to a knee-jerk response invented for just such an occasion. With as much sincerity as I could muster, I uttered the infamous: "I was only joking!"

Yeah, right. Leslie and I both knew I hadn't been joking. It's one of the oldest tricks in the book. Literally. Solomon must have heard it used plenty to have written this proverb.

For centuries, then, we humans have figured that if we could convince a friend or our spouse that a harmful comment was meant as a joke, we'd be off the hook. After all, laughter is good medicine (see Proverbs 17:22). It's true. In addition to laughter's positive biological effects—stimulating endorphins, lowering our blood pressure and heart rate—laughter simply improves our mood and increases our sense of belonging. No doubt about it, joking around is good for the soul, and even better for a marriage.

But when a spouse tries to gloss over a hurtful remark with the "I-was-only-joking" line, it's like shooting arrows at our spouse. And it's downright deceitful.

Far better than trying to cover the mistake, is offering a simple apology: "I'm so sorry."

ⵣ To Ponder ⵣ

- Have you ever caught yourself trying to deceive your partner by playing the "only joking" card? If so, what was the result?

- What are you doing to bring constructive, happy, healthy humor into your marriage?

3

A re Y ou Listening?

He who answers before listening—
that is his folly and his shame.

—Proverbs 18:13

J (Les) recently talked with a man who'd seen a demonstration of a remarkable new product—a universal computer that can translate from one language to another at a rate of a thousand words per minute.

The demonstration involved two couples conversing long distance. One couple was from Africa and spoke Swahili. The other, standing by their igloo in Alaska, spoke Klinget. As the couples spoke, they smiled in understanding and appreciation as their words were translated instantly and flashed upon the bottom of a life-sized split screen that showed both couples.

The problem occurred when the African man used an idiomatic expression to compliment the wife of the Alaskan gentleman. He said that she looked like a bird—high praise in Swahili. However, when it was translated, the message came through, "Your wife looks like a pigeon."

The Alaskan man scowled until the machine straightened out the translation and he understood the intended meaning—his wife was beautiful, like the most lovely bird in

Africa. At that point, my friend told me, the couples' expressions began to glow. They understood each other.

Understanding, whether it be across continents with different languages or across the kitchen table with different perspectives, is the bridge we build from our hearts, and it cannot be constructed quickly, not even with a high-powered computer. Of course, that's the temptation, especially in marriage. We want to build an expedient bridge to our partner's pain, or happiness, as the case may be. But understanding—which can only come through patient listening—can never be rushed. Martin Luther King, Jr., once said, "Shallow understanding from people of good will is more frustrating than absolute misunderstanding from people of ill-will."

How many times have you heard your partner describe a predicament—a mishap at work, a problem with the kids, a misunderstanding with a friend—and proceeded prematurely to solve his or her problem? You laid out three easy steps to clean up the whole mess, checked it off your evening's to-do list, and got ready for dinner. Husbands, in particular, seem compelled to fix their partner's problems, but the truth is, men and women are equally guilty of this marital mishap.

So the next time you are tempted to fix or explain away your spouse's problem, remember the words of this proverb: "He who answers before listening—that is his folly and his shame." In other words, listen to your partner as if you were from two different continents.

❦ To Ponder ❦

- Answering before truly listening is one of the easiest communication mistakes we make in marriage. Why do you think this is so?

- What are the practical communication tools you use to understand your mate? How can you put them into practice the next time you are tempted to answer before listening?

4

Wise Up

The fear of the LORD is the beginning of knowledge,
but fools despise wisdom and discipline.

—Proverbs 1:7

In Cincinnati, a man hired a helicopter to drop twenty-five hundred carnations and ten thousand love letters onto the lawn of a women he loved. Apparently the woman failed to share this man's affection, and she had him charged with littering. She told reporters he had "lost his mind."

Losing one's mind is a common danger in new love. The compelling emotional force of love can override the capacity to think clearly, and drive a person to become "crazy in love." And what's more, when one person's romantic passions are appreciated and returned by another, wisdom is all but put on ice. Once the spark of attraction between two people catches flame, love quickly turns into a raging, out-of-control fire. Engulfed by its heat, the couple becomes oblivious to sound judgment.

But even after the heat dies down and a couple settles into the comfort and warmth of a healthy marriage, there is no guarantee of sound judgment returning. The dizzying experience of early romance and the honeymoon period of marriage may have disappeared like a dream, but knowledge and wisdom do not automatically fill the void.

For this reason, God calls every couple to wise up. The Hebrew root word translated as "wise" or "wisdom" occurs more than three hundred times in the Old Testament. And in the Greek New Testament, "wisdom" is found more than sixty times. It is a word that implies having special knowledge and sound judgment: a wise carpenter is one who knows his trade well and makes good decisions. A wise couple is one who knows marriage well and works together on important decisions such as financial management and child rearing. According to the *American Heritage Dictionary*, wisdom is "a common sense understanding of what is true, right and lasting." Did you catch that? It is built on common sense. Unfortunately for many couples, it appears that Horace Greeley was right when he said, "Common sense is very uncommon."

Wisdom doesn't necessarily come with age or experience. Wisdom comes from the good sense to understand what is true, right, and lasting—it comes from "fearing the Lord." Seeking God is the starting point of all wisdom.

There is a small church in our neighborhood that understands the source of wisdom. Every year around Christmastime they display a rather shabby sign with an insightful message: "Wise men still seek Him."

So do wise couples.

❧ To Ponder ❧

- According to Proverbs, those who ignore wisdom forgo protection and will almost assuredly bring disaster on themselves. What examples of this truth, in the context of marriage, come to mind?

- "A prudent question," asserted Francis Bacon, "is one-half of wisdom." In other words, when we admit we need help, we become wiser. In what ways are you asking questions as a couple?

5

Being Your Partner's Publicist

*Let another praise you, and not your own
mouth; someone else, and not your own lips.*

—Proverbs 27:2

English author Samuel Butler once said, tongue in cheek, "The advantage of doing one's praising for oneself is that one can lay it on so thick and exactly in the right places." I know what he means.

Maybe it's because I had two older brothers to compete against, but I grew up with a compulsion to blurt out my own self-praise: "Did I tell you about my promotion?" "Did you know I met with the governor?" Leslie, on the other hand, is quite the opposite, rarely bringing extra attention to herself.

As you might imagine, our polar differences in this area have caused some inner reflection. And after more than a dozen years of marriage, each of us is beginning to find a better balance. I have a way to go, but I'm not as self-promoting as I used to be. And inch by inch, Leslie is getting a little more comfortable discussing her accomplishments when appropriate. But above all, we are learning to practice the proverbial secret of affirmation: Let another praise you and not your own mouth. This truth may not have been written with couples in mind, but the wise husband and wife will see its applicability to marriage.

In social situations it's often all too easy to tell loving couples from warring ones. Almost everyone has been at a party where one half of a couple has taken a public jab at the other. Perhaps it was along the lines of, "I keep wishing John would get out of his recliner, turn off the television, and help me out in the yard like he promised!" It's a bad idea to use the cover of an audience to say something you wouldn't say in private. Couples who can't contain their criticisms in public are in serious trouble.

Loving couples, on the other hand, use every opportunity to boost each other in front of other people and to cast each other in the best light—much as they did in their courting days, when they wanted their friends and family to like their new love. They say things like, "Sarah just got a promotion, but she won't tell you that." Or, "Rick may not mention it, but he secured a huge grant for his company this week." Loving couples praise one another in private and in public. They tell each other's stories of accomplishment.

So when you have an opportunity to bring praise to yourself in a social setting, skip it. But when an opportunity arises for you to compliment your spouse in front of others, don't let the opportunity slip by.

🌿 To Ponder 🌿

- On the continuum of bringing attention to yourself, to desperately trying to avoid it, where do you fall? How about your spouse? What are you each doing to help one another out with your differences?

- William Shakespeare said, "I will praise any man that will praise me." Do you ever feel like that? Are you willing to praise your spouse without an ulterior motive?

6

Yakety Yak

The wise in heart accept commands,
but a chattering fool comes to ruin.

—Proverbs 10:8

Leslie: The duffel bag from Les's last trip to the gym is half unpacked on the bed. Two pairs of tennis shoes are in the middle of the floor. Four days' worth of socks, T-shirts, and shorts are piled on a chair. The temptation is to describe every element of Les's sloppiness to him in hopes that this will make him clean it all up quicker. But that's a mistake.

Les: We're running late for a departing flight at the airport, the car is packed and ready to go, but at the last minute Leslie insists on putting one more outfit into the luggage— "just in case." The temptation is to tell her how, where, what, and why this is a big mistake, in hopes that she will stop dead in her tracks so we can hit the road. But that, too, is a mistake.

We've learned it the hard way. We are often tempted to dwell on problems in marriage rather than solve them. We throw out commands: "You better do this," or "You can't do that." We want to hash out every detail of why our partner is doing something they shouldn't, or not doing something they should.

The real way to make progress when faced with a problem, however, is not to dwell on it by pointing an accusing finger, but to solve it by proposing a commanding solution. Proverbs says a wise heart accepts commands. This does not mean that we have the right to order people around imperiously in order to solve our problems. Rather, the proverb implies that the wise person is more likely to hear a thoughtful, commanding solution than to listen to a "chattering fool" who simply talks on and on, criticizing and nagging.

Interestingly, *command* and *commend* come from the same Latin root. And as any successful commander knows, orders are more likely to be followed when a person is also commended, that is, when they are praised for their successes and good efforts.

So be sure to learn this lesson. Rather than bluntly pointing out foibles, temper your comments with a commanding solution. When your husband has made a mess with his dirty clothes, say something like, "From the looks of your duffel bag, you must have had a great week at the gym! But could you help clean up the bedroom now?" Or when your wife wants to pack just one more outfit and you are running late, you might say, "You'll look great in what we've already packed; are you sure we should risk missing our flight to pack one more thing? Couldn't you go without it?" In other words, make a request instead of dwelling on the problem. The wise person will hear the "command" in these recommendations, and, more likely than not, accept them.

🌿 To Ponder 🌿

- Think of the last time you were troubled by something your spouse was or wasn't doing. How did you attempt to cope with the problem? Did you chatter on about his or her error, or make a "commanding" solution?

- Most marriages have repetitive squabbles—irritations that happen again and again. What are yours? And what can you do the next time one of these arises so that you focus on a solution rather than dwell on the problem?

7

Truth or Consequences

A false witness will not go unpunished,
and he who pours out lies will not go free.
—Proverbs 19:5

He lied. She lied. Not a little lie, like denying that he ate the last chocolate chip cookie. Or pretending she loved the hot pink scarf she got for Valentine's Day. And not a huge, marriage-crushing lie, like having an affair.

He lied about working late when he was out with his buddies from the office. She lied about forgetting to drop off some dry cleaning that was supposed to be ready by the weekend. He lied about the price he paid for his new golf club. She lied about all of the bills being paid, when in fact the checkbook balance didn't cover the deficits.

If your spouse had been honest, you might have been hurt or angry, you might have had a fight or a long talk. But you almost certainly could have lived with the truth.

What you can't live with is your spouse's lying to you. You wonder: How could he or she pull such a sleazy maneuver? If my partner lied about this, what else might he or she lie about? How can you ever trust your spouse again? You thought you had an open, honest relationship, and now you feel like it's a sham.

When a partner lies to you, it's natural to feel as if the whole relationship has been called into question—because, in a sense, it has. But before you let suspicion tear the two of you apart, take some time to look for the larger truth behind the lie—the truth about you, about your partner, and about what you really expect from each other.

It may be, for instance, that while you give lip service to the value of honesty, the two of you have colluded to set up a marriage that actually encourages lying. This can happen when you try to preserve the perfect, unrealistic world of romance you had as a dating couple, insisting that the marriage remain endlessly loving, fun, tranquil, nonthreatening. Over time, it can seem as if neither one of you will tolerate anything less—won't tolerate, in other words, the truth.

Before you finger your spouse as the villain, ask yourself if you might be his or her accomplice, if both of you might use lying to sidestep hot issues and trouble spots. Examine whether his or her lie might be a way to shore up some basic insecurity in you or in the relationship.

We can become so intent on maintaining a reputation of selflessness or being in control and always right that we not only lie, we sometimes lie about lying: "I must have forgotten to mention I was going to a movie with my friends." Or, "I'm sure I told you. Maybe you blocked it out, honey."

If this sounds familiar, you've got to decide if protecting your egos is more important than protecting your marriage. And that decision is easy if you understand the clear message of this proverb: Deceit never goes unpunished.

❦ To Ponder ❦

- How much honesty do you truly want from each other?

- Humorist Franklin Adam was known for saying, "Too much truth is uncouth." Do you see any relevance for this statement in the marriage relationship? Can there be too much truth in marriage?

8

Yield in the Name of Love

*An offended brother is more unyielding
than a fortified city, and disputes are like
the barred gates of a citadel.*

—Proverbs 18:19

There is no way that I am going to spend sixteen hours in a car just to see your brother and his family for a day and a half," Janet declared.

"Well, I am not going to waste my vacation days sitting around a hot swimming pool doing nothing," Neil shot back.

Neil and Janet didn't see eye to eye. They were sitting in our counseling office trying to decide how to spend their vacation when this conversation erupted. They both had made up their minds, dug in their heels, and weren't budging.

We've seen a lot of couples hit this kind of brick wall. And we've certainly bumped our heads on it a few times ourselves. Compromise, yielding to another's wants, just isn't in our nature. But for a marriage to survive, the practice of compromise needs to be cultivated.

Loving couples negotiate. They talk through something to find a mutually satisfying compromise. It's not that hard, really. You probably did it without thinking when you were dating and oh-so-willing to consider the other person's wishes.

That's how you ended up having milk shakes at McDonald's after attending the ballet.

In a study of couples, Pepper Schwartz, author of the book *Peer Marriage*, found that among couples who enjoy equality in their marriages, there's less of the rank-pulling and power-playing so often seen in unhappy unions. Schwartz reports that these egalitarian twosomes have conversations filled with what she calls "tag questions," such as "Do you agree?" and "What do you think?" These little questions open the conversation to the other person's views, in much the way two business people who respect each other might interact. These equal partners hash out a fair agreement on anything important, from day care for the kids to what kind of vacation they will take. "Our solemn oath is: Never give up, never walk out—until we are both satisfied," one woman in a peer marriage told Schwartz. Pretty wise, wouldn't you say?

Winston Churchill once said, "The English never draw a line without blurring it." That should be true of the couple who learns to compromise. When a husband and wife come to believe that equality means splitting things precisely down the middle, then marriage becomes a contest of who can get a better deal. And that wipes out the true spirit of compromise. Finding an agreeable solution to disagreements means that sometimes one or the other partner gets a bigger piece of the pie.

Janet and Neil finally arrived at a compromise with their summer vacation—this year is with Neil's family, and next year at a sunny resort. Like all growing couples, they learned that both sides win when the lines are blurred and no one is keeping score.

🌿 To Ponder 🌿

- When was the last time you made an honest effort to compromise? What were the results?

- Read Proverbs 18:19 again. How does a marriage without compromise become as unyielding as a fortified city or as resistant as the barred gates of a citadel?

9

Right Here, Right Now

*Do not boast about tomorrow, for you do not
know what a day may bring forth.*

—Proverbs 27:1

For six years of graduate school I (Les) had a small sign pinned on a cork board above the desk where I spent most of my time. It was a quote from Abraham Maslow: "Some people spend their entire lives indefinitely preparing to live."

Hardly a week went by that I did not ponder that statement and desperately try not to focus all of my energy on the future. I needed that little reminder because I often felt as though my life was on hold—like someone had pushed the pause button—until I completed my degree. *After graduation*, I would tell myself, *we'll move into a bigger apartment . . . we'll take a long vacation . . . I'll have a real job with normal hours . . . I'll eat better . . . we'll go out on more dates . . . .*

After graduation, however, it wasn't long before I found myself saying, *once I get tenure as a professor . . . once I finish writing this book . . . once we own our own house . . .* and on and on.

It's tempting to boast about tomorrow. After all, the future holds many exciting possibilities. But when we focus our attention on what is around the corner, we miss out on what we have right now. And that is particularly true in marriage.

We often plan the perfect romantic evening in a candlelit restaurant, for example, and miss out on the loving moment in the glare of sunshine on our own doorstep. That's inspired marriage experts to label the greetings and good-byes we have with our mates as the most important moments of the day.

When a husband and wife come together after an absence—upon waking, getting home from work, or returning from a trip—the first few minutes will set the stage for how the rest of the time will go. Family therapist Marcia Lasswell says, "It's very important that the first few minutes of reconnection be positive and supportive. We all know how good it feels to walk into someone's presence and have them look up and smile, and how awful it is if he or she is preoccupied or negative." We know this because the "It's-good-to-see-you" look is what we instinctively gave, and received, in the early stages of our dating relationship.

So boast about tomorrow if you must, dream big dreams about your future, but don't forsake right here and right now. Your marriage will thank you.

🌿 To Ponder 🌿

- French philosopher Albert Camus said, "Real generosity towards the future lies in giving all to the present." Are you tempted to give more to the future of your marriage than you are to today?

- What can you do to remind yourself that the seemingly insignificant greetings and good-byes you have with your spouse are the most important moments of the day?

10

Building a Bridge Between Mars and Venus

There are three things that are too amazing
for me, four that I do not understand: the way
of an eagle in the sky, the way of a snake on
a rock, the way of a ship on the high seas, and
the way of a man with a maiden.

—Proverbs 30:18–19

Few books in recent years have been more popular than John Gray's *Men Are from Mars, Women Are from Venus.* And few books have been able to distinguish some of the most fundamental differences between men and women more clearly than this best-seller. When it comes to styles of interaction, for example, it really does feel as though the genders are from totally different planets. "Not only do men and women communicate differently," writes Gray, "but they think, feel, perceive, react, respond, love, need and appreciate differently."

"Great," you say. "We're from different planets. Why not just throw in the towel?" Some do just that. But other men and women manage to communicate quite well with each other. How do they do it? The secret is in understanding—and truly respecting—our gender differences.

Let's look at some of the most global differences between men and women. Of course there are always exceptions, but research and experience have revealed this fundamental difference between the sexes: Men focus on achievement, women focus on relationships. Sure, this is overly simplistic, but it's a place to start. In her groundbreaking book *You Just Don't Understand*, Deborah Tannen explains that men focus most of their communication on "report talk" (gathering information) while women focus on "rapport talk" (building camaraderie). However the big differences are labeled, they cannot be ignored.

In our own marriage, we have found that when we come to understand and accept our differences, we can avoid some of the biggest pitfalls of marriage and begin to reach out to each other in new ways. We can fine-tune our interactions as we come to learn about and understand our gender uniqueness.

Yes, we will always be different, to one degree or another. But once we've studied and accepted those differences instead of getting defensive about them, we build a bridge between Mars and Venus and make the mystery of our different planets less puzzling.

To Ponder

- While understanding some of the global differences between men and women is important, it is even more critical to study the unique differences between you and your partner. Have you done this? What are some of them?

- In his book *As for Me and My House*, Walter Wangerin writes, "Unless you learn to play a duet in the same key, to the same rhythm, a slow process of disengagement will wedge you apart, first secretly, psychologically, and then openly and miserably." What are you doing to play a duet in the same key with your spouse?

11

Hear No Evil, Speak No Evil

Without wood a fire goes out;
without gossip a quarrel dies down.

—Proverbs 26:20

You told Rich *what?*" Leslie exclaimed.

"Oh, he doesn't care if you lost fifty dollars," I said defensively. "If you didn't want me to tell him, you should have told me it was private."

"Excuse me," Leslie retorted, "but can't you just assume I don't want everyone to know my stupid mistakes?"

Good point. All of us talk with friends about our marriages, whether we tell our best friend everything or simply throw into conversation an occasional, "I know what you mean—Tim does that too." But what you *don't* tell your friends about your marriage is just as important as what you *do* tell them.

Protecting your spouse's confidence is critical to building a trustworthy marriage. Unfortunately, some couples become contaminated by gossip. Not shop gossip. Not party gossip. But gossip behind a partner's back about the state of the relationship. "I probably shouldn't even be telling you this but . . ." "Sarah would kill me if she knew I told you this . . ." "You won't tell Bob I mentioned this, will you?"

51

Some couples leak secrets and blab private information without a second thought. *Why*, you might well ask, even if you, yourself, are guilty of it. For several reasons. First, they see gossip as a means to connect with others. Being able to give someone the inside scoop can bring two people closer together. The gossip believes the person he or she is confiding in will feel privileged to know just how tough things are at home. Another reason for blabbing is a more destructive one: gossip can be used to get back at a mate. If a husband, for example, has confessed a struggle with pornography to his wife in an attempt to overcome it, and the wife feels betrayed and wounded as a result, she may tell her friends about it as a way of hurting her husband, or as a way of gaining power.

Whatever the reason, gossip is evil. The apostle Paul warns about the destructive power of gossip and the condemnation that comes to "gossips and busybodies" who say "things they ought not to" (1 Timothy 5:13). But this doesn't stop gossips. They don't even realize the damage they are doing to themselves, their mate, and their marriage.

Think of the remarkable energy that would be restored to a marriage if the partners "gossiped" about good things instead of bad. If, for example, a wife confided in a friend how sweet her husband was to clean up the kitchen. Or if a husband told a friend how generous his wife was in giving to the needy.

If you are ever snared by the grip of gossip in your own marriage, consider gabbing about the good. Leave the secrets at home and never betray a confidence.

❦ To Ponder ❦

- Are you tempted to gossip about your spouse or the state of your marriage? If so, what motivates you to do so?

- If you are on the receiving end of gossip about someone else's marriage, what can you do to cut it off at the pass?

12

The Purpose-Driven Marriage

Let your eyes look straight ahead, fix your gaze
directly before you. Make level paths for your feet
and take only ways that are firm.

—Proverbs 4:25–26

We recently celebrated our twelve-year wedding anniversary in the mountains of Colorado. This was not a camping trip, however. We were going deluxe: a late morning brunch, a lazy afternoon by the pool, maybe a little window shopping followed by a gourmet dinner. Well, that was the first day. When the second morning rolled around, we were ready for a change of pace. We wanted activity, an outdoor adventure. The night before, on our stroll through town, we spotted a mountain-bike rental shop. It had dozens of bikes with fat, knobby tires for traversing rocky terrain. So after a quick breakfast, we beelined it for the bikes, mapped out a route, and took off for the wilderness.

One thing we didn't consider, however, was the high altitude's impact on our breathing. Add to that the steep inclines, muddy patches, and crooked trails, and you can probably figure out that we did not get too far on our journey. We ended up returning to town and riding our bikes on paved, flat roads along the river. Ah, the serenity of a level path. No more huffing and puffing.

Proverbs has a lot to say about the benefits of traveling on a straight and level path. And so do we, especially when it comes to marriage. Of course, no marriage is exempt from a few steep inclines and rocky terrain. There will always be quick and unexpected turns. But we can do more than we think we can to smooth out the journey.

Proverbs speaks about "looking straight ahead" and "fixing our gaze." This is the talk of having a purpose, of having a mission. Have you ever considered establishing a marital mission statement that's unique to you as a couple? "Understanding that only God meets all our needs, we will love each other with empathy and try to model a healthy relationship to the young couples we mentor." That's part of our marital mission. At least for now.

Some of the most advanced corporations revisit their mission statement every few years. They study the document that sets forth their original aims, and then measure their performance. They determine whether the aims of the business have fallen out of sync with its mission statement, whether these aims need to be brought back into line, or whether the statement itself needs to be rewritten to reflect current realities.

The equivalent in marriage would be for a couple to repeat or revise their wedding vows every few years. When children enter the picture, a major job change occurs—any sudden turn in the road is reason to fix our eyes once again on the mission. When we do this, Proverbs says, we will walk securely and make a firm, level path for our feet.

To Ponder

- Have you ever worked on constructing a mission statement for a company or an event? Did you see the benefit? Why or why not?

- What do you think about your wedding vows serving as a kind of mission statement for your marriage? If you were to write your own marital mission statement, what would you include?

13

Turbo Talk

Do you see a man who speaks in haste?
There is more hope for a fool than for him.

—Proverbs 29:20

The scene? Our counseling office. The clients? Rick and Amy, a married couple of less than a year.

"I hear the words coming out of your mouth, but I just don't understand what you mean!" Rick's frustration was unmistakable. "It's like you're speaking a foreign language."

"Well, you're the only person I've ever known who didn't understand me when I talked," she replied angrily.

"What you say sometimes just isn't logical," he countered.

"I'm not like you, Rick, analyzing everything, picking apart every word." Amy was close to tears.

"I know. I just wish you weren't so emotional when you talk. I can't get what you're saying. We just can't communicate."

That's it, the number one complaint in marriage: We just can't communicate. The truth is every couple communicates whether they want to or not. Saying nothing is communicating. What most couples mean by this complaint is that they don't understand one another.

Like Rick and Amy, many of us have difficulty merely talking to each other from time to time. He answers a question simply and succinctly; she says he's not "listening" to her. She tells him she knows exactly how he feels; he thinks she's trying to one-up his experience.

In order to communicate more effectively with your partner, you first have to slow down. Good communication takes time. When the best-selling business book *The One-Minute Manager* was popular, there were a hundred spin-offs, including "The One-Minute Marriage." Give me a break. Maybe managers can accomplish their goals through quick contacts, but a husband and wife? Not likely.

When we slow down the conversation with our partner, we are less likely to give hasty orders and snappy solutions. When we slow down, we are more likely to listen to the emotions that underlie the verbiage of our partner's expressions and pay more attention to the nonverbal messages. These qualities help us avoid foolish conversations and bring about true understanding.

So slow down. Allow your mate time to mull things over if he or she needs it. Don't rush to fill in the silences. Talking can happen on the run, but understanding takes time. Listen to the wise message of Proverbs: "Do you see a man who speaks in haste? There is more hope for a fool than for him."

❦ To Ponder ❦

- James 1:19 says "be quick to listen, slow to speak." That can be a tough assignment. How are you practicing it in your own marriage?

- Recall the last time you or your partner jumped to a conclusion or gave advice without understanding the issue. What was the result?

14

A Kinder, Gentler Marriage

An anxious heart weighs a man down,
but a kind word cheers him up.

—Proverbs 12:25

Spouses routinely underestimate the importance of a kind word. We're not talking about elaborate praise or a heartfelt poem, as wonderful as these things are. We're talking about the simple, everyday kindness of small talk. "Thanks." "You're great." "I missed you today."

"The small day-to-day things you say are more important than any of the overarching communication issues," says Clifford Notarius, author of *We Can Work It Out*. Most marriage experts agree. Thomas Holman, a professor of family sciences at Brigham Young University who studies ways to increase marital quality, has found that making time for small talk is at least as important to couples' happiness as agreement on values and role expectations, demographic similarities, emotional health, or parents' marriage success.

When a couple is just sitting around talking, one of the things they are saying is, "You are important enough to me just to sit here with you." It's what Dr. Holman calls a "Maxwell House moment" because it is the kind of casual exchange that usually takes place over a cup of coffee. The subject isn't relevant; it's the kind words and the time spent together that matter.

Each of us needs someone to listen to the little everyday aspects of our life, like how irritated you were in the school parking lot or how friendly the person you met at the grocery store was. When you chime in with the occasional "uh huh" or "really?" you're showing that you care not just about the chitchat at hand, but about the speaker, your spouse. And that's good for the soul. It calms our anxious heart and cheers our heavy spirit.

If good everyday communication sounds simple, it is. It's great if you learn the good active-listening skills and speaking skills that we therapists emphasize. But what's most important is that you simply have the ability to show love, appreciation, caring, and concern enough to have warm conversations with each other.

So the next time your spouse has a heavy heart, remember that you don't have to throw a party, buy presents, or hire a clown. All you need is a kind word.

🌿 To Ponder 🌿

- Have you ever considered the importance of everyday chitchat to your marriage? What are you and your partner doing to build in a daily routine of Maxwell House moments?

- Too often, married couples let communication fall by the wayside. The television or the newspaper becomes a barricade to kind small talk. Do these kinds of things interfere with your marriage?

15

A Penny Saved Is Sometimes Chintzy

Do not eat the food of a stingy man,
do not crave his delicacies; for he
is the kind of man who is always thinking
about the cost. "Eat and drink," he says to you,
but his heart is not with you.

—Proverbs 23:6–7

No, really, go ahead, order whatever you want," I told Leslie.

We were sitting in an upscale restaurant perusing the menu when she said something about the grilled tuna looking pretty good. *I hope you're not being serious*, I thought. *That dish is the most expensive thing on the menu.* I didn't want to come off as miserly in such a nice place, but I also didn't want to break the bank on a single meal.

I was panicky. So, in the meekest tone I could manage, I asked, "Are you sure you wouldn't like one of the pasta dishes?"

I kept my eyes fixed on the menu as I asked the question, but I could feel Leslie eyeing me to get a read on my unspoken intentions.

"Sure, the pasta primavera looks pretty good, too," she said without revealing a twinge of disappointment.

Phew, I could relax again. It looked like I wasn't going to have to fork out *too* much money. It was about that time, however, that the waiter arrived:

"Can I start you off with something to drink?" he asked.

"Just water for me," I blurted out, hoping Leslie would catch the cue.

"You know," Leslie told the server, "I think I'll have an iced tea."

"What?" I exclaimed as soon as the waiter was out of earshot. "Do you know how much that's going to cost?"

"I thought you said to order whatever I wanted," Leslie innocently replied.

She caught me red-handed. I did say that. The problem was I didn't mean it. I didn't mean it at all. I wanted her to order the cheapest thing she could find. And once my selfish desires were exposed, I felt like crawling under the table.

Have you ever felt that way? I didn't want to be stingy. I wanted to be a nice guy. I just didn't want to pay the price, that's all. The problem is that being generous always requires paying a price. That's what journalist Sydney Harris was getting at when he said, "People who think they're generous to a fault usually think that's their only fault."

I could rationalize my stingy ways by saying I was only being prudent so we could enjoy even more fine dining, and that might be true. But managing one's pocketbook without regard for one's partner is missing the point. As this proverb says, no one wants to dine with the man who says, "Eat and drink," but his heart is not with you.

Is there a place for being prudent, frugal, and thrifty with the one we love in marriage? Sure. But only when careful ways are outweighed by generosity to overflowing.

🌿 To Ponder 🌿

- Think of a time when you were being a bit more chintzy with your partner than you needed to be. What was the result and was it worth it?

- Samuel Johnson once wrote, "I do not call a tree generous that sheds its fruit at every breeze." What do you suppose he meant by that, and how might it relate to generosity in marriage?

16

Compromising Positions

When pride comes, then comes disgrace,
but with humility comes wisdom.

—Proverbs 11:2

$\mathcal{I}$t's my way or the highway." Ever felt like that? Of course you have. We have all had times where we wanted something done our way while our spouse wanted it done another.

Make way for compromise—not one of my favorite words. I (Leslie) view it much the way I view such things as sit-ups and checkbook balancing: necessary but evil.

Some people start out marriage thinking they shouldn't have to compromise because they should agree on everything. That's because during courtship they *seem* to agree on everything. But over time, different needs and issues are brought to bear. And if a husband and wife don't learn to eat a little humble pie and make some compromises now and then, they might as well give up. Marriage cannot survive without compromise.

Let's define our terms here. For something to qualify as a compromise, both people involved have to give a little something that's of consequence to them. It's not a compromise if you're giving up something you don't view as important at all.

For the most part, I'm pretty amiable. It's all the same to me whether our vacation is a rugged camping trip in the woods or a stay at a luxury resort. It's all the same to me if we have pasta for dinner, order in Chinese, or open a can of soup. Therefore, my going along with Les's preferences on these matters doesn't really count as a compromise.

On the other hand, there's coffee. I love Starbucks coffee. I stop at nearly every Starbucks that's open, day or night (and where we live in Seattle, that's a lot of stops). In fact, these days, with our heavy travel schedule, I have even conditioned Les (who is not a coffee drinker) to stop at the airport's Starbucks for me before we even check in at the ticket counter. So if Les asked me to go without Starbucks for any reason, I would definitely be making a compromise. Get the difference?

Arriving at a mutually pleasing compromise doesn't only solve an immediate, specific problem, it also ushers in a spirit of humility to the marriage. You see, selfish pride is the primary barrier to compromise in marriage. And when we compromise, humility is infused into the relationship. No wonder Proverbs states that when pride enters the picture it's a disgrace, but humility cultivates wisdom.

🌿 To Ponder 🌿

- When was the last time you allowed selfish pride to seep into your marriage? What was the result?
- Humility often means having to say, "I'm sorry." Do these words roll off your tongue or get stuck in your throat?

17

Raging Passion

*A fool gives full vent to his anger, but a wise
man keeps himself under control.*

—Proverbs 29:11

Several years ago I (Les) attended a workshop promoting a new therapeutic tool to help people manage anger. It was a foam rubber bat designed for hitting something—or someone—without causing harm or pain. The idea was that an angry person in a counseling office could blow off steam, or "vent" anger, by physically hitting the object of his frustration.

Nothing could have been more damaging than this silly exercise in physical combat. I have worked with enough angry people in therapy to know that while helping them to get in touch with buried anger can serve a useful purpose, expressing it frequently and openly neither removes the cause of anger nor drains away the feelings of frustration. In fact, plenty of research now shows that "ventilation" techniques only reduce one's control against anger, and encourage more frequent and aggressive forms of the behavior.

When we practice letting angry feelings out, we become less able to control them the next time. Rather than "ventilating" the emotion and getting rid of it, we find it returns more frequently. And, like a muscle that we exercise over and over again, those feelings we "exercise" become stronger too.

The author of this proverb, better than any modern day psychologist, understood how anger works. "A fool gives full vent to his anger," he wrote, "but a wise man keeps himself under control." How can we do this when feelings of anger become overwhelming? We do it by making a simple distinction between feeling angry and behaving angrily. The apostle Paul understood this when he said, "In your anger do not sin" (Ephesians 4:26). Paul is saying that the feeling of anger itself is not wrong, but acting out the anger can lead to serious problems. In other words, as long as you recognize the anger as your own and avoid hurting the object of your anger, you are keeping it as a feeling—and that's legitimate. What you do with your angry feelings, however, may not be. Far better than lashing out in anger is talking it out. You may need some distance to get anger under control (a long walk sometimes helps), but this beats venting every time.

Anger in marriage, especially when we nurse it, motivates us to wound and perhaps even despise our spouse. We cannot love under these conditions, and everything we stand for is in danger of being destroyed when we allow anger to be transformed into hostile words and actions.

❦ To Ponder ❦

- Are you a volcano, building steam and ready to erupt with anger? If so, what are you doing to keep it under control?

- Author Louisa May Alcott said, "It takes two flints to make a fire." What do you make of that? If your spouse is about to blow his or her stack, do you take any responsibility for it? Is this the right thing to do?

18 🌿

Eat, Drink, and Be ... What?

Better a meal of vegetables where there
is love than a fattened calf with hatred.

—Proverbs 15:17

"Pass the corn."

"Where's the salt?"

"Move over."

"Do you have to chew your ice so loud?"

These are just a few of the common utterances around most family dinner tables. Pleasant, huh? And too bad. Mealtime offers one of the best opportunities for human connection and companionship—especially for couples. Culinary writer M. F. Fisher is known for saying, "Sharing food with another human being is an intimate act that should not be indulged in lightly."

The writer of Proverbs would certainly share M. F. Fisher's sentiment. You can have a dinner table with every delectable delicacy and the bounty of each season, but if the emotional tone around the table hangs heavy with unpleasantness, you might as well be eating leftover pizza from somebody else's party: "Better a dry crust with peace and quiet than a house full of feasting, with strife" (Proverbs 17:1).

Think about it. The usual scenario is that two people reunite at dinnertime and grouse to each other about the events of their day: "Traffic was terrible on the way home tonight." "Did you pick up my dry cleaning?" "Your mother called again." "I need the car tonight." Or, even worse, they flip on the television and eat without saying a word. Such "absent but present" level of communication is not necessarily harmful. It's just that the potential for meaningful connection is being missed. And the more frequently mealtime is taken for granted, the farther a couple drifts apart.

If you want to reclaim table time with your spouse, make it a pleasant time that both of you look forward to. You don't have to cook like Julia Child or set a table like Martha Stewart to make mealtimes pleasurable. What matters most is the focus of your conversation. Don't allow it to be a time of dumping your problems on your partner. When your spouse asks you how your day was, even if it was horrendous, say, "I'll tell you in a minute, but right now it's good to be home with you." Set the tone for an evening that will be uplifting, spontaneous, and positive. Give your partner your attention before you give him or her your problems. "Let your conversation be always full of grace, seasoned with salt" (Colossians 4:6).

❧ To Ponder ❧

- Describe a typical dinner scene in the home you grew up in. What was the conversation like?
- What can you and your partner do, in specific terms, to make your mealtime more pleasant?

19

Hope and the Hurting Heart

Hope deferred makes the heart sick,
but a longing fulfilled is a tree of life.

—Proverbs 13:12

Last night I talked with a close friend whose marriage is hanging in the balance. His wife has already divorced him emotionally, and her filing for the real thing seems almost inevitable. "How do you stay so positive?" I asked him.

"It's not easy," he replied, "but it's because I still have hope."

Hope. What a powerful human attitude!

Our hearts still become heavy under the burdens of our lives, but hope keeps our head up. For most of us, the aching our heart experiences when we are coping with the pain of a difficult marriage drives us to lose hope of ever having our longings fulfilled.

Most couples in trouble think that for things to improve, extraordinary changes, if not a miracle, have to take place. And human nature being what it is, many of us who have relationship troubles think these changes need to be made by our spouse, not ourselves. But we often don't acknowledge that we have no control over our partner's behavior.

As a result, we develop a sense of hopelessness and helplessness about the relationship. The breakthrough comes when we realize that by making even small changes in ourselves—avoiding criticism of our spouse, affirming the positives, and so on—we can effect big, positive changes that make us more optimistic. We need optimism to help us fulfill our longings. Hope is what regenerates our vision and gives us perseverance.

Poet Emily Dickinson once wrote:

"Hope" is the thing with feathers—
That perches in the soul—
And sings the tunes without the words—
And never stops—at all—.

If you are barely hanging on to hope in your marriage, don't give up. As hopeless and helpless as you may feel, you can still sing a few notes of the marriage song. The music doesn't depend entirely on your partner. The small changes you make in yourself really can bring about big changes in your relationship and move you further from a "hope deferred" and closer to a "longing fulfilled."

❧ To Ponder ❧

- Think of an experience where you gave up hope. How did your passive resignation affect the situation?

- If your marriage is fulfilling and in good shape, you probably still know someone whose marriage is on the rocks. What can you do to help them not give up hope?

20

Money Matters

> *Honor the LORD with your wealth, with the*
> *firstfruits of all your crops; then your barns will*
> *be filled to overflowing, and your vats will brim*
> *over with new wine.*
>
> —Proverbs 3:9–10

When my husband and I agreed that I should quit my job to stay home with our daughter," Jenny confided in us, "our income suffered an incredible hit. And at the beginning of each month, Dan and I nearly came to blows ourselves. We'd just look at that huge pile of unpaid bills, and we'd start to fight."

Interestingly, Jenny told us that they had argued about money even before she quit her job. "It really doesn't matter how much we make or who makes it," she said. "Dan insists that I am irresponsible with money, and I maintain that he is a miserly doomsayer."

Sound familiar? Money is the number-one issue couples fight about. Since financial decisions have to be made almost daily, they are frequent fodder for fights. And many underlying emotional issues can cause money battles. Sometimes it's power and control. Sometimes the fights stem from the partners' differing family backgrounds. What's surprising to many couples is that money fights are not a function of how much money you have or don't have. It has more to do with the attitudes each of you bring to money itself. And the more important money is to you—whether you are a hoarder or a spender—the more likely you are to have fights about it in your home.

Therefore, one of the best-kept secrets to financial success in marriage is found in this proverb. It has to do with recognizing money's power. You see, money is very alluring and deceiving. And when our greed is seduced, money becomes a mistress. Paul saw this fact when he observed that "the love of money is a root of all kinds of evil" (1 Timothy 6:10).

Every marriage must protect itself against greed and self-centered consumerism. And one of the best ways to do this is to give money away. That's right, give it away. This proverb is urging us to do so: "Honor the LORD with your wealth, with the firstfruits of all your crops." God has given us all we have. And by giving a portion of what he has given us back to him, we free ourselves from its tyranny.

The Bible calls us to "profane" the god of money by giving it away. And to do that, we must take Christ's famous exhortation and apply it to our checkbooks: "For where your treasure is," Jesus said, "there your heart will be also" (Matthew 6:21).

❦ To Ponder ❦

- English philosopher Francis Bacon said, "Money is like muck, not good except it be spread." Do you agree? Why or why not?

- Consider the last tussle you and your partner had about money. What was the real issue? Would it have been different if each of you had approached it with the attitude of honoring the Lord with your wealth?

21

Getting It Straight

Trust in the LORD with all your heart
and lean not on your own understanding;
in all your ways acknowledge him, and
he will make your paths straight.

—Proverbs 3:5

Because of the work we do with engaged couples, we attend a lot of weddings. Sometimes we feel like we have seen or heard of everything you could possibly do to make a wedding ceremony memorable and special. But not long ago we discovered something we had never seen before, and it impressed us.

You have probably seen the use of a unity candle where a couple joins two individual candle flames together to light a larger candle, symbolizing their union. Well, in this case, the symbolism went much deeper. Our friends Jim and Jeannette wanted something that would express their trust and dependence on God in their marriage, so they came up with what they called the "unity cord."

Standing before the congregation, they braided three cords together, symbolizing the powerful strength of their marriage when they lean not on their own understanding but on the wisdom of God. The three separate cords represented the three participants in this lifelong union—Jim, Jeannette, and God's son, Jesus Christ. By the braiding of these three cords, Jim and Jeannette visually illustrated their new oneness, intricately interwoven and strengthened by their love of God. The minister explained that the braided cord was far stronger than either of the individual cords representing Jim and Jeannette had been. He then read from Ecclesiastes 4:9–12:

> *Two are better than one,*
> *because they have a good return for their work:*
> *If one falls down,*
> *his friend can help him up.*
> *But pity the man who falls*
> *and has no one to help him up!*
> *Also, if two lie down together, they will keep warm.*
> *But how can one keep warm alone?*
> *Though one may be overpowered,*
> *two can defend themselves.*
> *A cord of three strands is not quickly broken.*

The message Jim and Jeannette conveyed in their wedding ceremony has become an inspiration to us in our own marriage and has called us to trust more deeply in the Lord and lean not on our own understanding. In trying to do this, we have discovered that the best route is to practice the message of this proverb: "In all your ways acknowledge him, and he will make your paths straight." When we acknowledge God's presence in our marriage, we are braiding our marriage with God's power.

❦ To Ponder ❦

- Trusting in God can be an abstract endeavor if you do not think about it in practical terms. What are you and your partner doing to trust God together?

- How do you interpret the part of this proverb that says when you acknowledge God he will make your paths straight? What does that mean to you?

22

Guard Your Heart

Above all else, guard your heart,
for it is the wellspring of life.

—Proverbs 4:23

Virtually every couple who takes the marriage vows fully intends to fulfill them. On their wedding day, most couples are not thinking of the "poorer" and "worse" and "sickness" parts of their vows. They're filled with hopes, dreams, and expectations. Eventually, of course, reality sets in, and they begin to live out the final phrase of the vows—sticking together until death parts them. That's when marriage gets dicey. That's when marriage needs protection.

Our society is full of people whose dreams of lifelong commitment have been shattered. But those who take their wedding vows seriously believe that a promise is made to be kept, till death. That promise is made not only with their heads, but also with their hearts.

Robertson McQuilkin, former president of Columbia Bible College and Seminary, is a powerful example of a promise kept. We told his story in our book *Saving Your Marriage Before It Starts*. When his wife, Muriel, was diagnosed with Alzheimer's disease, McQuilkin faced two divine callings: president of two schools and husband of Muriel. He couldn't do both, but it took "no great calculation," as he put it, to resign his position and give himself to caring for Muriel. He believed it was a matter of integrity. Forty years earlier he'd promised to care for his wife in sickness and in health. "She's such a delight to me," he said. "I don't *have* to care for her, I *get* to!"

What a remarkable statement: I don't *have* to, I *get* to! What a remarkable heart! When it comes to tough times, our natural tendency is to ask, "What's in it for me?" "How will I benefit?" But the moment we ask these kinds of questions is the moment our heart is unprotected and vulnerable to excessive self-indulgence. Our self-centered desires sabotage our heart's capacity for commitment, and we instinctively look for the easy way out, the path of least resistance. And that path always leads to heartache.

No successful marriage has made it on the well-worn path of selfishness. Successful marriages occur when two partners guard their hearts from selfish ways and forge a new and noble path of other centeredness. On this path you will find yourself saying, "I don't have to, I get to." On this path, you find "the wellspring of life."

So guard your heart.

❦ To Ponder ❦

- Have you ever found yourself asking the question, what's in it for me? Most of us have. What can you do to guard your heart against such a selfish motive in marriage?

- Do you know of other stories like the one of Robertson and Muriel McQuilkin? What do couples like this do to protect their hearts from selfish motives?

23

Two's a Couple, Three's Therapy

*Pride only breeds quarrels, but wisdom is found
in those who take advice.*

—Proverbs 13:10

We can usually spot the uneasiness the moment a couple walks into our office. They sit uncomfortably on opposite ends of the couch and look as though they are about to be grilled like flank steak.

One of them, usually the husband, doesn't want to be there. He's never been in a place like this before, he doesn't know what to expect, and he's agreed to come only because his wife has dragged him. She, on the other hand, wants to be there. And she specifically wants him to be there. She knows a bit more about what to expect but still has trouble finding a way to start. She looks at him. He looks at the floor. Finally it falls on us to break the silence.

"So," we will say, "what brings you here?"

It's a good question even though we can pretty much predict the answer. They are there, in a therapist's office, for the same reason every other couple is: They want to know how they can make their relationship work. And in some cases they want to know if their relationship is going to make it at all.

But couples therapy, or just plain good counsel from a wise friend or mentor, isn't only for embattled spouses. What used to be a last resort, in fact, is now an increasingly popular option for any state of a marriage. Counselors who used to focus exclusively on the make-or-break variety of interventions are now equipping themselves for doing basic marriage tune-ups on successful relationships. And with good reason. There is so much good research and information on marriage just sitting around waiting for real-life couples to put it to good use.

But while going to counseling is becoming less of a stigma, far too many couples allow pride to stand in the way of receiving a bit of advice. It seems many couples would rather have their fingernails pulled out than visit their local marital therapist. I suppose this shouldn't be too surprising when you consider that therapy demands emotional vulnerability, not to mention the admission that you can't solve every problem by yourself. That's especially difficult for men. After all, men are socialized to repress feelings of hurt, shame, or caring. Push a young boy into the playground dirt, and he knows it's his job to come back with a fistful of gravel, not a face full of tears.

Whatever the aversion to counseling may appear to be, pride is almost always a factor. That's why this proverb says, "Pride only breeds quarrels, but wisdom is found in those who take advice."

❧ To Ponder ❧

- Have you ever sought the help of a professional counselor for marriage advice? If so, was overcoming pride an issue in getting you there? If not, was pride a factor in keeping you from it?

- If you want to seek marriage counseling but your spouse is resistant, how might you make the whole process less threatening?

24

Time to Heal

Each heart knows its own bitterness,
and no one else can share its joy.

—Proverbs 14:10

*O*n my (Leslie's) parents' thirty-fifth wedding anniversary, our family suffered a meltdown.

Dad was a well-liked pastor, low-key and hardworking. Under his leadership congregations grew and deepened their faith. His ministry was marked by serenity, a rich investment in relationships, and a nonflashy style of teaching and preaching. But after what must have been a strained and eerie anniversary dinner, Dad told Mom a secret he had been keeping for months, disclosing a decision no one would have predicted. After thirty-five years of ministry and marriage, he was calling it quits. Dad was having an affair, and he didn't want it to end. The next day he turned in his ministerial credentials, moved in with his secretary, and walked away from his former life.

Devastated and in agony, Mom was left alone to pick up the pieces. She was in fragile health with severe diabetes, but always faithful, invested in her marriage, and obedient to God. She had been a committed partner in ministry and never imagined that adultery would shatter her world.

Neither did I. *How could Dad leave?* I asked again and again. *This goes against everything he ever taught me! Doesn't he see the incongruity of his decision?* Questions like these pummeled my mind. One day I cried for eight hours without stopping. That was several years ago, and today the healing is still not complete. On occasion, the same questions pierce my stillness, and the tears flow freely.

When Les and I first learned of my father's affair and his decision to leave my mom, we were on vacation far from home. Disbelief and sheer shock is the only way to describe our reaction. The next day we flew home, where our shock turned into anger, followed quickly by concern for Mom's survival. "Mom has lost everything," I told Les, "her marriage, the parsonage, her income—everything!" The crisis consumed me. I could think of nothing else.

We went on with our lives—teaching, writing, grocery shopping, watching television, crawling into bed at night. But what had happened would not leave my mind. Les never had to ask me what I was thinking—he knew. He patiently listened to expressions of my breaking heart. He absorbed every painful and ugly feeling he could. Even months later when there were days as dark and tearful as the first one, or when I just couldn't decorate our home for Christmas because of painful memories, he never panicked or demanded that I pull myself together. He held me gently, listened, and gave me comfort. But no matter how caring Les was, I still felt alone. He can never fully know the pain of my heart. As the proverb points out, "Each heart knows its own bitterness."

But given time, marriage cuts our personal pain in half. And even when it may have seemed impractical and indulgent to do so, Les gave me time to heal. And this gift brought a balm of understanding to my spirit. As another proverb (14:29) says, "A patient man has great understanding."

🌿 To Ponder 🌿

- Think of a time when your personal pain was so great that your partner could not fully enter in. Were you and are you, in spite of the loneliness, able to accept this as reality?

- When your partner is in pain, a pain you cannot fully comprehend, what can you do to increase your understanding of it?

25

The Wife of Your Youth

May your fountain be blessed, and may you
rejoice in the wife of your youth.

—Proverbs 5:18

Romeo and Juliet didn't get many votes at all. Neither did any of the currently hot, young couples in Hollywood. The couple that most closely models ideal love, according to two hundred fifty participants in an America Online poll, is actor Hume Cronyn and the late actress Jessica Tandy. In a sex-crazed, age-allergic society, their enduring love and marriage over several decades won out over all-consuming passion.

When the survey asked what makes love last, the answers included having a child together, buying a home, and commingling finances. Shared religious convictions carried more weight than shared political views.

The survey also revealed that romance doesn't have to be expensive. Most respondents preferred a bouquet of wildflowers, picked spontaneously, over a dozen roses. A candlelit dinner at home won out over dinner at a fancy restaurant. And if you really want to show how much you love your partner, respondents suggested taking care of a chore that he or she usually has to do.

The ideal day of romance, according to survey results, included breakfast in bed, a picnic in the country, or an elegant dinner. Jacuzzis figured prominently in the responses. So did the element of surprise and the absence of interruptions. One woman said her ideal day of romance was simple: "He'd never call his office or take calls on his portable phone."

The message is clear, men. We don't have to be a Mel Gibson or a Brad Pitt to make love exciting. We don't have to spend money like Donald Trump to be romantic. Women admire enduring love over all-consuming passion, time and again. They aren't looking for expensive preprogrammed evenings. They'll take the spontaneous heartfelt gesture of love every time.

So I ask you: What are you doing to rejoice in the wife of your youth? Remember her? She's the woman with whom you patiently picked out a china pattern before you got married. The woman for whom you wrote poetry or planned a surprise trip to the zoo. The woman who took priority over every work deadline and all other appointments. This is the wife of your youth. Remember? And according to Proverbs, it's time you got reacquainted. Listen to these wise words from Solomon (Proverbs 31:10–12): "A wife of noble character who can find? She is worth far more than rubies. Her husband has full confidence in her and lacks nothing of value. She brings him good, not harm, all the days of her life."

Let's be honest, men. If we have found a noble wife, we are blessed. And it's time to rejoice in our blessing.

❦ To Ponder ❦

- When was the last time your wife took priority over a project at work or an "important" deadline? All the time, you say? Does she feel the same way?

- In practical and concrete terms, what can you do this week to celebrate the wife of your youth?

26

A Husband's Crown

A wife of noble character is her husband's crown,
but a disgraceful wife is like decay in his bones.

—Proverbs 12:4

In the 1930s he was the world's most eligible bachelor, attracting adoring females wherever he ventured. The courtly Prince of Wales was born and bred to be the King of England, but he was still unmarried at age forty-one. His detractors said he was weak-willed and incapable of making up his mind. But when the man destined to be crowned Edward VIII came to a decision, it was a big one.

On December 11, 1936, in a radio broadcast heard by millions, the newly proclaimed king announced the unthinkable. "I have found it impossible to carry the heavy burden of responsibility and to discharge my duties as king as I would wish to do," he said, "without the help and support of the woman I love." That woman was a twice-divorced American named Wallis Simpson.

Although this wildly romantic declaration cost Edward his job and his country, for the king it seemed an even exchange. "She promised to bring into my life something that wasn't there," he explained in his autobiography. "I was convinced that with her I'd be a more creative and more useful person."

By many accounts, however, Wallis never really wanted to marry the king. She was content with the status quo and had in mind, according to Donald Spoto, author of *The Decline and Fall of the House of Windsor*, being a royal mistress. Besides, as head of the Church of England, the king is forbidden to marry a divorcée, and it never occurred to Wallis that Edward would exchange the monarchy for marriage. But this didn't stop Edward from declaring: "The throne means nothing to me without Wallis beside me." His brother, father of the current queen, was crowned George VI five months later.

Before they even married, according to Spoto, Wallis Simpson "was bloody bored with the king and wanted out . . . but he threatened to commit suicide and she was cornered." The couple married six months later in a borrowed chateau in the Loire Valley before only sixteen guests. The life that followed was empty. They lived in voluntary exile in Paris. "You have no idea how hard it is to live out a great romance," Wallis told a friend.

I am sure Lady Di and Fergy would agree. Fairy tale romance is just that—a fairy tale, not reality. King Solomon, of noble lineage himself, surely understood the heartache of trying to live a storybook existence. Faraway castles, beguiling jewels, and even surrendering the throne for love are only an illusion of real life romance. A husband's true crown, according to this proverb, is "a wife of noble character." This is the only authentic and healthy way to live out a great romance.

How does a woman become a wife of noble character? The answer is found in another proverb (31:30): "Charm is deceptive, and beauty is fleeting; but a woman who fears the

LORD is to be praised." Fearing the Lord—it is a phrase that appears numerous times in Proverbs and throughout the Bible. It means showing reverence for our Maker and being in awe of God. It means loving God with all our heart, and all our soul, and all our mind.

❦ To Ponder ❦

- Most of us idealize great love stories. We envision only the most romantic moments. Why do we do this, and how might this tendency harm our own marriage?

- What can you do to become a spouse of noble character? In practical and concrete terms, how can you "fear the Lord" and so become your partner's crown?

27 🌿

Smart Lips

The lips of the righteous nourish many,
but fools die for lack of judgment.

—Proverbs 10:21

A friend of ours, recently divorced, was sitting in our living room one evening after dinner. We were talking about a new book on some heady subject, a book I had not read. Les was explaining the author's newfangled view on human intelligence when I spoke up to clarify some perfectly meaningless point of fact.

"I saw part of an interview with the author on the news, and I didn't get the impression he was saying it the way you are," I told Les.

"Have you read the book?" he countered.

"No, but I'm pretty sure you are wrong on this."

For several interminable minutes we debated the author's message, becoming increasingly tangled in our positions, until some still-sane remnant of my character wondered why it was so important that I win this argument about nothing.

I looked at our friend, the survivor of an unhappy marriage and a cruel divorce. She was smiling, and I asked her why. "I just remembered why I'm glad I'm not married anymore," she said.

Ugh. Les and I looked at each other sheepishly. How foolish! How insensitive! Oh, sure, a little squabble never hurt anyone, and after all, isn't being genuine vitally important? But this was neither the time nor the place. We apologized to each other and to our guest and spent the rest of the evening trying to put the best face we could on marriage. We wanted our friend to know that marriage is not about being beaten down, it's about being built up. It's about being strengthened and nourished—even when we discover ourselves in the midst of an inane conflict.

Since that night in our living room, we have tried to use better judgment—especially in front of the engaged and newly married couples we know and work with. Not that we are now staged or artificial. We don't script our dialogue or plan our conversations. We simply are who we are, but with better judgment. We try to live out this proverb by speaking in ways that nourish and strengthen our own marriage as well as others'.

You may be surprised by the inspiration and uplift that comes to you and to others when you consider living out the words of this proverb: "The lips of the righteous nourish many, but fools die for lack of judgment."

☙ To Ponder ☙

- Have you ever considered how your marriage, the way you live it out, impacts other couples? How about how you impact your single friends' attitude toward marriage?

- Have you ever had an embarrassing marital moment in public that did not "nourish" the people around you? What can you do to improve the situation if you find yourself in this kind of circumstance?

28

No-Fault Marriage

Do not accuse a man for no reason—
when he has done you no harm.

—Proverbs 3:30

Virtually every couple we see in therapy is interested in what, or who, caused their problems; they're looking for a place to lay blame. What they do not understand about problems in marriage, technically speaking, is that causes are not simple matters. Finding fault—in the truest sense—is not easy. Why? Because the influences on a problem are reciprocal. They cannot be pegged on one thing or one person.

One of the most profound secrets of human relationships we know is this: Causality is circular. In a marital problem, choosing the point at which the causal chain begins is pointless and arbitrary. There is no one single cause for anything in marriage.

Does that make you feel uneasy?

Most of us are far more comfortable with a linear cause-effect approach where an unhappy childhood or bad nerves can explain undesirable behavior. The truth is that human relationships are not that simple. A better approach is to focus not only on what goes on inside a person, but also on what takes place between two persons.

When two individuals come together in a marriage, something is created that is different from, larger than, and more complex than those two individuals apart. In psychobabble terms, we call it a *system*. And the most important feature of a system is communication.

Relationships are established, maintained, and changed by what and how we communicate. Over time, we establish patterns for communicating that become habitual and enduring. We fall into a groove without even giving it conscious thought. When Leslie is late, I whine, she feels rejected, and to protect herself she blames me for being uptight. This repeated conversation creates a pattern—I am increasingly anxious about Leslie's inability to be on time, and if she is running late, she is likely to delay even more in order to avoid my whining.

Our spouse's actions depend upon ours, and vice versa. In a system, all elements are mutually dependent. In other words, unless you decide to change the system, you are not acting on your own free will. You are constantly being influenced by your partner.

Here's the good news. A marriage is not a static and fixed relationship. No matter how entrenched one's behavior or how strong one's personality, each individual is influenced by the other on an ongoing basis. So here's the clincher: Once you recognize your partner's dependence upon your pattern of behavior, you can consciously plan and change your own behavior, thereby influencing your partner and improving the relationship. It's like a marital dance.

The point is that no one is really to blame in a marriage relationship. Both of you have established your routine. And by heightening your self-awareness of the patterns in your relationship, you will learn what moves you can make to positively affect your marriage—without playing the blame game.

❧ To Ponder ❧

- It's so easy to find fault and lay blame. What can you do, in practical terms, to avoid this easy temptation in your own marriage?

- When you have been blamed by your partner, how do you feel? Does it motivate you in a positive direction? Why or why not?

29

You Haven't Got Time for the Pain

*Hatred stirs up dissension, but love covers over
all wrongs.*

—Proverbs 10:12

It hadn't been a good morning. Just before breakfast they had blown up at each other.

"You are so self-centered and insensitive," she told him.

"Well, you overreact to everything," he retorted.

She wanted to take some time to talk about the situation. He couldn't get out of there fast enough. Before they hopped in separate cars to drive to work, each got in a few final jabs on the fly.

Truth be told, the argument had been building up over several weeks, maybe even months. Linda thought about all the times Ron was preoccupied with his job, his friends, his hobbies, his favorite team—anything but her. She began to wonder, "Does he really love me anymore? If he really loved me, would he treat me this way?"

Ron was irritable when he got to work that morning. "What's gotten into Linda?" he wondered. "She's really turned into a nag—just like her mother!"

That morning both Ron and Linda felt terribly alone. They both wondered if they were going to make it as a couple. With their hurts running so deep, their marriage loomed over them like an endurance contest.

Have you ever felt that way? If not, you have certainly felt the stinging pain, if only briefly, of something your spouse said or did. With marriage comes pain. It's part of the package. And, whenever we are hurt, we usually see ourselves as innocent victims. Someone has done us an injustice, and now we're left to pick up the pieces. While it's true we may be victims, we are not *helpless* victims. We can choose how we'll respond. We can either choose to be angry, self-righteous, and resentful, or we can choose to rise above the negativity, forgive whoever hurt us, and move on.

That's what this proverb is all about: forgiveness. Unless we live in total denial, it's the only way to cover over all wrongs. And it begins when we free ourselves from any vindictiveness and desire to hurt back. "Do not repay anyone evil for evil . . . do not take revenge," says Paul in Romans (12:17–19).

We can't change our spouse. But we can change our attitude. And we do that by surrendering the opportunity to hurt our spouse when he or she hurts us. That's forgiveness. And it covers over all wrongs.

🌿 To Ponder 🌿

- Jesus set forth a powerful principle in forgiveness when he described "turning the other cheek." In a sense he is saying, "When someone hurts you, you are better off letting him hurt you again than trying to hurt him in return." Are you able to do this with your spouse (barring any physical or verbal abuse)?

- Your spouse has caused you pain. There is no way around this in marriage. But you don't have to hold on to the pain. Are there hurts in your own marriage that are particularly difficult for you to let go?

30

The Mosquitoes of Marriage

A fool shows his annoyance at once,
but a prudent man overlooks an insult.

—Proverbs 12:16

You really look tired," I said to Leslie as we climbed into the car to run a quick errand.

"What do you mean by that?" Leslie snapped.

"Just what I said," I countered. "I know you haven't gotten much sleep, and it shows."

"Well, I'm not tired," Leslie declared, "and I find your comment very insulting."

Ever had one of these "insulting" conversations? They're a little like trying to swat mosquitoes. The insults are not very big, but the more annoyed you get with them, the more irritating they become, and the more difficult they are to squelch. These annoying conversations are not uncommon in marriage. After all, when a man and a women live under the same roof and spend time together, insults—intentional or not—are bound to occur.

Happy couples, however, have learned the wisdom of this proverb. When one partner feels that a comment could have been meant as a zinger, he or she makes a decision to overlook it and move on. Think of the excruciating time this saves and the hassles it avoids! To overlook a potentially harmful word is key to avoiding countless annoyances and building a happy marriage.

Not surprisingly, research has recently backed up what this proverb has proclaimed for three thousand years. Blaine Fowers at the University of Miami has studied what he calls "marital illusions"—the fantasies and unrealistic ideas people hold about marriage in general and their partners in particular. And he's found that happy couples are more likely to form illusions than unhappy couples. They agree to unrealistically rosy descriptions of their marriage. And they idealize their spouses, attributing more positive qualities to them than to anyone else and giving their spouses credit for more positive aspects of the marriage than themselves.

In other word, the higher a couple's capacity to overlook potentially harmful words, the more marital satisfaction they enjoy. It makes good sense. As Proverbs 11:27 says, "He who seeks good finds goodwill, but evil comes to him who searches for it." If you are looking for an insulting word from your spouse, give it time, and you will probably find it. But if you're looking for goodwill from your partner, sidestep the annoyances, and focus on the compliments. You'll be surprised by the number you find.

🌿 To Ponder 🌿

- It is so difficult to overlook something that hurts our feelings. The benefits, however, far outweigh the effort. How can you do this more frequently in your own marriage?

- When was the last time you overlooked an annoyance from your spouse? What was the result?

31

Are We Peers Yet?

As iron sharpens iron,
so one man sharpens another.

—Proverbs 27:17

The headline of a recent *Seattle Times* article caught my (Leslie's) attention. It asked a seemingly innocent question of married couples, "Are we peers yet?" Searching for clues about my own marriage, I decided to take the ten-question "mini-diagnostic test" that promised to tell me if my own marriage was, in fact, a "peer" marriage (between equals), a "near-peer" marriage (where equality is admired but still out of reach), or a "traditional" marriage (where a hierarchy establishes the husband at the top). The mini-test consisted of questions about who initiates sex, who controls the money, whose career is given prominence, and the role each partner takes as a parent.

Sociologists willingly acknowledge that there are many ways to make a marriage work, but marriages between equals or peers are thought to be more satisfying to both partners and make for a mutually more satisfying relationship. However, according to sociologist Pepper Schwartz, author of *Peer Marriage: How Love Between Equals Really Works*, only ten to fifteen percent of all American couples live in a peer marriage. Would my self-test reveal that I was one of the lucky few?

The idea of being a peer with my husband has always been important to me. When he decided to pursue a doctorate, we made the decision together that I would also pursue a doctorate, in large part, to protect the peer quality of our relationship. In our twelve years of marriage we have coauthored books, cotaught courses at the university where we both work, and generally approached our lives as a team. But the questions on this test made me doubt my equal footing. How could I be certain that I had an equal say in how we spend our money? In a crisis, would my voice really carry the same weight as his? The test revealed that my marriage was more near-peer than peer, but it was the questions more than the results of the test that got me thinking.

Later that day, as Les and I opened our mail over peanut butter sandwiches at our kitchen table, I unrolled a mental tape measure on our relationship. Determined somehow to quantify and compare the power each of us had in the marriage, my attitude resembled that of the finicky building inspector who had approved our home loan. I wanted to uncover any faulty wiring or unstable structures that could dismantle our peer rapport.

Before I had finished my sandwich, however, I realized that my inspection was misguided. Who in our marriage was initiating or controlling this or that didn't really matter to me. The true measure of a peer marriage, I believe, is not so much power as it is a spirit of reciprocal respect and dedication to the partnership. Whether you are in a peer, near-peer, or traditional marriage—based on how you answer a list of ten questions—isn't really the point. What matters is less measurable and objective. It's whether you are peers of the heart, equally dedicated to the well-being of the marriage and improving one another—just as iron sharpens iron.

❦ To Ponder ❦

- How do you and your partner stack up as peers: "traditional," "near-peer," or "peer"? What difference does your standing make in your marriage?

- What are you doing as a couple to sharpen one another, to improve and grow as individuals?

Epilogue

As we stated at the outset, the Old Testament book of Proverbs serves an undeniably positive function for couples willing to learn its wisdom. And in this little book of meditations we have selected a few of those wise sayings which have particular relevance to marriage. But there are hundreds of other practical proverbs for couples in this ancient book of learning. So in closing this selection of meditations we urge you to search the book of Proverbs for yourself. Discover practical wisdom in the form of poems, parables, and couplets. But most importantly, apply God's wise counsel to your marriage.

Love's Unseen Enemy

How to Overcome Guilt to Build Healthy Relationships

Dr. Les Parrott III

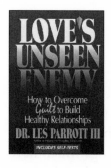

Too often efforts to build loving relationships are unwittingly sabotaged by an unseen enemy: guilt. In *Love's Unseen Enemy*, Dr. Les Parrott shows how to build healthier relationships by overcoming the feelings of false guilt and by dealing forthrightly with true guilt.

Dr. Parrott identifies the four relationship styles created by the combination of love and guilt:

- **Pleasers** love with their hearts, not their heads. They do loving things to relieve their guilt.
- **Controllers** can identify the problems with their minds, but don't always exude warmth and love.
- **Withholders** carry their guilt but are afraid to love.
- **Lovers** have learned to tap their capacity for genuine empathy. They strive to be loving, not simply to do loving things.

Parrott shows how your relational style affects your friendships, your marriage, your children, your work, and your relationship with God. Look for *Love's Unseen Enemy* at your local Christian bookstore.

Love's Unseen Enemy
0-310-40150-X Hardcover

ZondervanPublishingHouse
Grand Rapids, Michigan
http://www.zondervan.com

A Division of HarperCollins*Publishers*

Becoming Soul Mates

Cultivating Spiritual Intimacy in the Early Years of Marriage

Dr. Les Parrott III and Dr. Leslie Parrott

Becoming Soul Mates gives you a road map for cultivating rich spiritual intimacy in your relationship. Fifty-two practical weekly devotions help you and your partner dig deep for a strong spiritual foundation in the early years of marriage.

In each session you will find:

- An insightful devotion that focuses on marriage-related topics

- A key passage of Scripture

- Questions that will spark discussions on crucial issues

- Insights from real-life soul mates like Pat and Shirley Boone, Zig and Jean Ziglar, and Tony and Peggy Campolo

- Questions that will help you and your partner better understand each other's unique needs and remember them in prayer during the week.

Start building on the closeness you've got today—and reap the rewards of a deep, more satisfying relationship in the years ahead. Pick-up *Becoming Soul Mates* at your local Christian bookstore

Becoming Soul Mates
0-310-20014-8 Hardcover
0-310-21926-4 Softcover

ZondervanPublishingHouse
Grand Rapids, Michigan
http://www.zondervan.com

A Division of HarperCollins*Publishers*

Saving Your Marriage Before It Starts

Seven Questions to Ask Before (and After) You Marry

Dr. Les Parrott III and Dr. Leslie Parrott

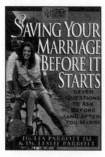

Did you know many couples spend more time preparing for their wedding than they do for their marriage?

Having tasted firsthand the difficulties of "wedding bell blues," Drs. Les and Leslie Parrott show young couples the skills they need to make the transition from "single" to "married" smooth and enjoyable.

Saving Your Marriage Before It Starts is more than a book—it's practically a premarital counseling session. A few questions that will be explored are:

Question 1: Have You Faced the Myths of Marriage with Honesty?

Question 3: Have You Developed the Habit of Happiness?

Question 6: Do You Know How to Fight a Good Fight?

Questions at the end of every chapter help you explore each topic personally. Companion men's and women's workbooks full of self-tests and exercises will help you apply what you learn. And the *Saving Your Marriage Before It Starts* video curriculum will help you to learn and grow with other couples who are dealing with the same struggles and questions.

Here's what the experts are saying about *Saving Your Marriage Before It Starts:*

"I've spent the past twenty-five years developing material to strengthen marriages. I wish Saving Your Marriage Before It Starts *had been developed years ago."*

H. Norman Wright
Author of *Before You Say I Do*

"The Parrotts have a unique way of capturing fresh insights from research and then showing the practical implications from personal experience. This is one of the few 'must read' books on marriage."

Dr. David Stoop, Clinical Psychologist, Co-host
of the New Life Clinics Radio Program

WINNER OF THE 1996 ECPA GOLD MEDALLION BOOK AWARDS

Saving Your Marriage Before It Starts
0310-49240-8 Hardcover
Saving Your Marriage Before It Starts Audio Pages
0310-49248-3
Saving Your Marriage Before It Starts Video Curriculum
0310-20451-8
Saving Your Marriage Before It Starts Workbook for Men
0310-48731-5
Saving Your Marriage Before It Starts Workbook for Women
0310-48741-2

ZondervanPublishingHouse
Grand Rapids, Michigan
http://www.zondervan.com

A Division of HarperCollins*Publishers*

Questions Couples Ask

Answers to the Top 100 Marital Questions

Dr. Les Parrott III and Dr. Leslie Parrott

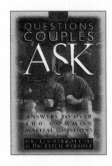

Ask yourself the following . . .

How can I be honest without hurting my partner's feelings?

What do we do when one of us is a spender and one of us is a hoarder?

What can we do to protect our marriage against extramarital affairs?

How can we be more spiritually intimate as a married couple?

From communication, conflict, and careers to sex, in-laws, and money, *Questions Couples Ask* is your first stop for help with the foremost hurdles of marriage. Drs. Les and Leslie Parrott share cutting-edge insights for the 100 top questions married couples ask. Whether you want to improve your own marriage or nurture the marriages of others, Christianity's premier husband-wife marriage counseling team equips you with expert advice for building a thriving relationship.

"Today's married couples find it hard to get the answers they need to their marital questions. They're often so overwhelmed that they don't even know what questions to ask. Les and Leslie Parrott give us the right questions to be thinking about—and the right answers."

— Dr. Robert G. Barnes,
Sheridan House Family Ministries

To find answers to these and many other martial questions pick up your copy of *Questions Couples Ask* at Christian bookstores near you.

Questions Couples Ask
ISBN 0-310-20754-1 SC

ZondervanPublishingHouse
Grand Rapids, Michigan
http://www.zondervan.com

A Division of HarperCollinsPublishers

The Marriage Mentor Manual

How You Can Help the Newlywed Couple Stay Married

Dr. Les Parrott III and Dr. Leslie Parrott

YOU CAN HELP NEWLYWEDS BUILD A STRONG, LASTING MARRIAGE

If you have built a strong marriage, you have a wonderful opportunity to pass on to other couples what God has given you. Part of the successful Saving Your Marriage Before It Starts program, *The Marriage Mentor Manual* shows experienced couples how they can mentor newlyweds during their first year of marriage.

"Marriage mentoring can be a significant help to building a lifelong marriage," say Les and Leslie Parrott. "We have seen hundreds of couples strengthen their new marriages through mentoring relationships and know firsthand how beneficial this relationship can be." *The Marriage Mentor Manual* shows you—

* Who are good candidates for mentoring relationships
* How to find and establish mentoring relationships
* How to be effective mentors and practice the art of active listening
* When to refer a troubled couple to a professional counselor
* What mentoring can do for you

With a year's worth of guidelines, exercises, and questionnaires, *The Marriage Mentor Manual* will help you encourage and strengthen couples who are just starting out—and improve your own marriage in the process.

Pick up your copy of *The Marriage Mentor Manual* at your local Christian bookstore.

ZondervanPublishingHouse
Grand Rapids, Michigan
http://www.zondervan.com

A Division of HarperCollins*Publishers*

The Marriage Mentor Manual
Softcover 0-310-50131-8

We want to hear from you. Please send your comments about this
book to us in care of the address below. Thank you.

ZondervanPublishingHouse
Grand Rapids, Michigan 49530
http://www.zondervan.com